The First Pressing

The First Pressing

Poetry of the Everyday

Donna Wahlert

iUniverse, Inc.
New York Lincoln Shanghai

The First Pressing
Poetry of the Everyday

All Rights Reserved © 2003 by Donna Wahlert

No part of this book may be reproduced or transmitted in any form or by any means, graphic, electronic, or mechanical, including photocopying, recording, taping, or by any information storage retrieval system, without the written permission of the publisher.

iUniverse, Inc.

For information address:
iUniverse
2021 Pine Lake Road, Suite 100
Lincoln, NE 68512
www.iuniverse.com

Special thanks to RoseAnn Wilgenbusch for the design of the cover and interior graphics, and to Louise Kames for her artistic technical help.

ISBN: 0-595-28959-2

Printed in the United States of America

Grateful acknowledgment is made to the editors of publications in which the following poems previously appeared. There may be slight changes in titles and format.

Ancient Paths, No. 3, Fall, 1999, *Separation*
Animal Blessings, June Cotner, HarperSanFrancisco, 2000, *Deer Domain* and *Blessings in All Direction* and *Animal Blessings for the Feast of St Francis of Assisi*
Baby Blessings, June Cotner, Harmony Books, 2002, *Colic* and *To My Eurasian Grandchild*
Bless the Beasts, June Cotner, Seastar Books, 2002, *The Mother Goose Prayer*
Christmas Blessings, June Cotner, Warner Books, 2002, *Gabriel* and *In China During Christmas*
Clarke College, Mary Blake Finan Literary Award, 1985, *Sonnet to My Daughter on Her Twenty-First Birthday*
Earth's Daughters, No. 47, 1996, *Wedding Cake*
Gulf Coast Chapter, National Writers Association, 1999 poetry contest, *I Come From a House With No Floors,* First Place Winner
Heal Your Soul, Heal the World, June Cotner, Andrews McMeel, 1998, *Windchimes*
Hidden Roots, Penhaligon Page Ltd., England, 2000, *You Herald A New Dynasty (To my Eurasian Grandchild)*
Kalliope Vol. XV, NO. 1, 1992, *Explaining to My Children*
Lifeboat: A Journal of Memoir, Leaving Home, Issue 1: Autumn, 2002, *Leaving This World For the Next*
Lyrical Iowa 1998, 53rd Annual Anthology, *Triolet to Spring (Triolet to a Spring Fawn),* Honorable Mention
Looking for God in All the Right Places, Loyola Press, October, 2003, *Windchimes*
Mediphors, No.4, Fall/Winter, 1994, *Colic.*

Mothers and Daughters, June Cotner, Harmony Books, 2001, *Attending the Birth of My Granddaughter* and *Sacrament* and *Before My Granddaughter's Surgery (Before My Grandson's Surgery)*
100 Words on Secret, University of Iowa, Vol. 3, No. 3, 1995, *Closing In*
Palo Alto Review, Spring, 1994, *Triolet to My Granddaughter (Triolet to Sydney)*
Poets On: Complaints, Issue No. 37, Summer, 1995, *Earthbound,* nominated for Pushcart Prize
Poets On: Twentieth Anniversary Reprise, Vol. 20, No. 2, Summer, 1996, *Earthbound*
Proposing on the Brooklyn Bridge, Poetworks/ Grayson Books, 2003, *Still Life*
Sistersong: Women Across Cultures, Vol. 2, no. 2, summer, 1994, *Novena*
Slant, Vol. 8, Summer, 1994, *Tea Time at Thomas Hardy's Cottage*
Thema, Vol. 5, No. 4, Summer, 1993, *Dust*
The Magnetic Poetry Book of Poetry, Workman Publishing, N.Y., 1997, *Dusk Lowers Its Scrim*
The Tucson Poet, Vol. 3, issue 2, winter, 1998, *The Jelly maker*
The Year 2000 Poetry Diary, Poetry Today, Penhaligon Press, England, 1997, *My Grandmother's Kitchen,* and *Reflection* and *Another Season,* and *Observing Thanksgiving* and *Here let Us*
Verve, Letting Go, Vol. 6, No. 2, Fall, 1994, *Generations*
Wedding Blessings, June Cotner, Broadway Books, 2003, *After Fifty Years (After His First Heart Attack)* and *Forty Years Are Not Enough*

This book is dedicated with great love and appreciation to

My darling husband, Bob

My children, Rob, Amy, Kathy, Marni and Mark
And their spouses

My thirteen grandchildren

My mother, Marge Allendorf, (1910-1999) who read to me endlessly

My father, Don Allendorf, (1910-1989) whose love for me was enduring

Table of Contents

Spring *1*
    Attending the Birth of My Granddaughter 3
    Triolet to a Spring Fawn 5
    Echoes 6
    Blessings in All Directions 7
    Eve 9
    To My Eurasian Grandchild 10
    Sacrament 11
    Before My Grandson's Surgery 12
    Triolet To Sydney 14
    Hanna 15
    The Mother Goose Prayer 16
    A Snake As A Pet 18
    Tea Time at Thomas Hardy's Cottage 19
    The Barometer Plunges 20
    Colic 21
    Deer Domain 23
    Putti 24
    First Communion 25
    Windchimes 26

Summer *29*
    We Have Moved To A New House 31
    A Three-Year-Old Visits 34
    Climbing Down the Rocky Mountains 35
    Flora 37
    Music to My Ears 39
    Separation 40
    Meditation at 7:00 a.m. 43

The First Pressing

Generations 44
The Transplant 45
God As Heat 47
Ballooning Over Minnesota 48
Making Way For the Interstate 50
Concerning Dogs 52
Evening Drama 54
Storm Signals 54
In The Garden With My Grandson 55
This Mississippi 56
An Astonishing Side Trip 57
Ode to Bread 58
Wedding Cake 59
East meets West 61
Nine-Eleven 63
Nocturne 65

Autumn **67**
Another Season 69
Windfall in the Orchard 71
Animal Blessing for the Feast of St. Francis of Assisi 73
Observing Thanksgiving 74
The Quilters 75
Sonnet To My Daughter on Her Twenty-First Birthday 76
I Wish I could Write a Poem About My Mother 77
My Grandmother's Kitchen 79
Blessing For Family Reunion 81
Novena 82
Dust 83
Old Loves Revisited 85
Go Figure… 87
Last Chance 88
I come from a house with no floors. 90
To A Lost Grandmother 92

A Catholic Woman Asks: Who is Priest? 94
Still Life 95

Winter *97*

Snowbirds 99
On Folding Napkins For a Dinner Party 101
When the Time Comes 103
Strands 104
The Jelly Maker 106
Lucy Conquers ALS 108
The Curtain Falls 109
In China During Christmas 111
Gabriel 113
Closing In 115
Untethered 116
After Life 117
Seasoning 119
Earthbound 120
Here Let Us 123
Between Two Worlds 124
The Long Good-Bye 126
Leaving This World For The Next 129
Reflection 131
Triolet to My Five Children 132
After His First Heart Attack 133
Forty Years Are Not Enough 134
After His Second Heart Attack: A Psalm 135
Upon Awakening 136
Explaining To My Children 137

Title Poem

Still Life

We have stretched past
our middle years, olive trees
ready for the late autumn pressing.

Our children are grown, ripe as Bosc pears.
Our grandchildren are in the vineyard
awaiting their first cutting.

Our fathers are asleep in the field.
Our mothers walk in the mist
toward the furrows.

Some of our leaves have faded;
some pile up on dried grasses.
But we still have patches

of cobalt green and yellow ochre
layered on us with a kind palette knife.
The light still comes from the east.

The First Pressing

We gently await
the artist's next brush stroke;
savoring this stolen season.

Preface

As my five children were leaving the nest, I returned to college and finished my degree in English. As a way of trying to understand this new emptiness and change in role, I began writing about the every day things, the tiniest moments in an ordinary life.

I attended poetry-writing workshops at the University of Iowa through the Summer Writing Festivals. In alternating years, I drove the nine hours to Duluth, Minnesota, for post-graduate study with internationally known poets, through the University of Minnesota's Splitrock Program.

Encouraged by these poet-professors, I submitted a few of my poems to editors. The first poem to be published was *Explaining to my Children*, in 1992. That kind acceptance was enough to encourage me to continue to send out my work again and again. Since then, I have been fortunate enough to have my poetry appear in about forty journals and anthologies. Affirmed by those who have read my work and attended my poetry readings, and in answer to their perennial question, "When are you going to publish your own Book?" I thought it was time to gather many of the poems and house them under one roof.

The poems that I have chosen for this slim volume speak about subjects as delightful as the birth of a grandchild or finding a newborn fawn at my front door; as varied as living with dust and selling wedding cakes. Some poems recount incidents on travels to England, Russia, and China. Others refer to living in Iowa and Florida; and some pine for both the Mississippi and the Gulf.

A son leaving for college, a daughter turning twenty-one, a daughter giving birth, a grandchild's surgery, a spouse's heart attack—all leave their emotional imprint on these pages. The same is true of events encompassing the larger world: the collapse of the Soviet Union, Tiananmen Square, Columbine High School, Nine-Eleven.

The First Pressing

Included are a handful of pieces tracing the progress of Alzheimer's disease; others face death and loss. In counter-point to these are easier themes of courting, marriage, mature love, and the grace of aging.

Whether poems describe children in apple orchards or snowbirds driving south or a hostess folding napkins for a dinner party or splashing a jigger of bourbon in a pumpkin pie, they are all the product of reflection, re-living the experience, and valuing the small transcendent moment that can become significant and eternal.

As I looked for a uniting theme and title for this book, I was drawn to my poem, *Still Life*, which appears on the previous page. This poem embraces the four stages of life: childhood, adulthood, middle years, and later years. In the poem, I have used the metaphor of the four seasons to describe these life markers. The book also does this and is divided into the four sections: Spring, Summer, Autumn, and Winter. The title was gleaned from the imagery in the first stanza.

> We have stretched past our middle years
> Olive trees ready for the late autumn pressing.

When I was searching for a title, I was in Florida, and 800 Black Olive trees were in bloom around me, nodding in the breeze. As I thought about olives and pressing them into oil, I realized that the first pressing produces the purest and best olive oil. I thought that maybe that image could work for these poems, written over fifteen years, and now gathered to go to press together for the first time in *The First Pressing*.

Just as the oil from the first pressing is pure and natural and the best—used for everyday things from cooking and burning in lamps to healing and anointing—I hope these poems, which speak of everyday things—are the best that I have to offer.

Donna Wahlert

Donna Wahlert

Note: Profits from this book will be used for the education, support, and respite for families whose loved one suffers from Alzheimer's disease

Part One

Spring

"I saw the spring fawn newly born
tucked under the yew bush at my front door."

Attending the Birth of My Granddaughter

I stood between the **O** of your mother's panting
mouth and the roundness of her belly.
Your father gripped her hand
at her thigh, bracing her bent knee
as she pushed you through that elastic circle.

We saw the roundness, the top of your head,
now a tiny ear, a chin, soft shoulder,
then your belly and cord and legs and toes
all there at once: ruddy, wiped off, clamped
off, handed off to your mother, your father.

I touched you, round under my hand.

Now I take my turn feeding you
at home on the sofa, under only a midnight moon.
The stripe of light falls across your face
catching your eyes, the **O** of your mouth,
slender fingers moving in shadow.

The First Pressing

I hold you up to the moon
like a shaman, like a grandmother.
I ask for health, wisdom, grace
to encircle your head, tiny ear, chin,
shoulders, belly, legs, toes—forever.

Triolet to a Spring Fawn

I saw the spring fawn newly born
tucked under the yew bush at my front door.
Spotted, he lay on smooth circles of river stone.
I saw the spring fawn newly born
signaling the end of winter's storm,
parable of a season whose possibilities we share.
I saw the spring fawn newly born
tucked behind a burning bush at my front door.

Echoes

I saw you four minutes
after your stubborn birthing
warming under nursery lights
eyes clamped tight, tugging at your hair
lips moving in silent chastisement
as if to scold for meddling with your fetal nap.

Two winters later, you visit
this sleepy gulf island
toddle across the strand
taste a pearl moon shell
rattle a sand dollar and chase
a string of scampering sandpipers.

Warmed by the noontime sun
eyes squinting against its flare
you again pull at your hair
jabber at the birds in disapproval
and echo that moment
when you were four minutes old.

Blessings in All Directions

I look to the north and see
hardy caribou, noble elk
the Husky, rolling in snow
the salmon struggling upstream to spawn
the deer whisking his tail with elegance.

I look to the south and watch
the alligator measuring the pond
the armadillo turning his armor to the world
the wings of pelican, wood stork, heron
catching the low warm air streams.

To the west is the
rim-eyed panda, the yak, the kiwi,
a koala nestled in the fork of a blue gum tree
the take-charge kangaroo and wallaby
leaping to attention, balancing the world on thick tails.

The red earth of the east
is the setting for the stately parade
of giraffe, elephant, gazelle,
fringed lion, svelte tiger, portly hippo—
all staking a claim for their home on the continent.

The First Pressing

I look nearer to home and glimpse
the curious Persian cat, the faithful Labrador,
the regal quarter horse
content gold fish, clever hamsters,
the reptile appreciating friendship.

As I finish taking inventory,
I send up a prayer of thanksgiving
for these blest animals, who reflect all of creation,
and who share with us
this air
this water
this dust.

Eve

In Hebrew her name was *hawwa*
Or *hayyim*, meaning life.
Through the millennia her name
has been transmitted, transmuted,
translated, and transcribed.

At the very beginning, Adam claimed her
and named her, "bone of my bone."
If he was a romantic, this first fellow
may even have called her, "heart of my heart."
Today, in honor of that first woman,

You are christened, "Eva Grace."
Your tiny voice is music eva-nescent;
your every movement eva-porates into dance.
You fill each dawn with newness eve-rlasting.
You end each day as quietly as Eve-nsong.

To My Eurasian Grandchild

You herald a new dynasty
not with thunder, sword
or purple robe;
but with birth pang,
cord and bone
and the swaddling clothes
of brotherhood and peace.

You hold the promise of
a fifth season, an eighth sea.
You join the richness of Renaissance
and the stature of Ming.
You are a thought breathed by the Buddha
a prayer whispered by the Christ.
You are a new moment of grace in the cosmos.

Written while rocking a newborn grandchild at 4:00 a.m.

Sacrament

I swaddle
    and rock you
my cheek
    to your brow.
We breathe grace
    to one another.
You leave your handprint
    on my soul
and with the balm
    of your baby scent
I am anointed
    as your grandmother.

Before My Grandson's Surgery

A thousand miles away from you
I do not know where to turn.
I visit the Trappestine Monastery,
then sit on a bench by their small lake.
I read, I pray, I contemplate.

An anhinga hangs from a fallen tree
drying out like a sail in the wind.
A snakebird darts under
the water like a crafty fish.
A salamander separates from his tail,
then scampers away.

Thoughts of you beat in me
like the snowy egret's wings.
I think of your tiny body,
that mite of kidney,
that thread of tubing tangled
like knitting yarn.

Donna Wahlert

These minutes, these hours hang
like that still anhinga. I want to dive
with you into the smooth cool lake.
I want us to separate from the pain
like the salamander. I want to run
with you to a safer place.

Triolet To Sydney

I remember your hand curled in mine
as you slept; your breath a refrain.
Tiny shoots of bone, nails opaline
I remember your hand curled in mine.
Your season budded newly green
Mine burned red with autumn in the vein.
I remember your hand curled in mine.
As you slept, your breath, a refrain.

Hanna

Solemnizing
Wedding vows
on their anniversary,
your parents
glowing,
minister praying,
family flanking,
friends smiling,
six tiny
cousins—
like angels
hovering—
breezed up
the aisle
with you
in a pillowed
flower-wrapped
brand-new
Red Flyer.
Hanna,
you were
a sacrament
in a wagon.

The Mother Goose Prayer

Written for the children's book: <u>Bless the Beasts:</u>
<u>Children's Poems and Prayers About Animals</u>

Dear God,
You protected the lamb following Mary to school
The mouse running up and down the clock
Even the cow jumping over the moon.

You took care of Mother Hubbard's hungry dog
The sheep munching in the meadow
The cow trampling the corn.

You soothed Miss Muffet's spider
Rescued the blackbirds in the pie
And sent the king's horses to mend
  Humpty Dumpty.

You comforted the three little kittens who lost
  their mittens
Listened to the cat with the fiddle
Guided the pussycat to London to see the
  Fair Queen.

Donna Wahlert

But I have this new kitten that needs
As much help as Mother Goose's pets.
Can you take care of him, too?

A Snake As A Pet

Snakes are said to crawl, slither, twist, and coil.
They're not like the furry dog
who tramps behind you
then settles faithfully at your feet;
nor the sleek cat who independently decides
to end his pacing and pads to your side;
not even like the fish who flashes back and forth
across the tank hoping to be hand-fed.

The snake
whose name was blackened in Eden,
who was cursed as the asp and adder,
who was conquered by Jason and the Argonauts,
who ended Cleopatra's queenly life,
entwines, encircles, embraces
just thankful to have a friend.

A scene witnessed in Higher Bockhampton, Dorset, England, 200 yards past the cottage where Thomas Hardy was born.

Tea Time at Thomas Hardy's Cottage

Beyond famed thatched roof
and wild garden flowers,
a dun-colored donkey trots along
a weathered wooden fence;
jogs directly to the Dorset farmer
reddened by wind and summer sun.
With quiet smile, the country man leans
into the rusty hinged gate
pats the beast's jowl
nuzzles his neck
with unshaven cheek.

Turning, he scoops up a handful of grain
cups it steadily, patiently,
until the large yellow teeth stop grinding.
He whisks his two hands together twice—
a signal that tea time has ended.
The donkey nods, turns, heads back to the moor;
the farmer returns to his work.

The Barometer Plunges

On the dawn of the day you were born
the sky mixed a new blue,
roused greening buds and lilacs
that shook their dew
onto bees unfolding their flowers.

By that afternoon,
deer eerily left the shadowed woods,
left hart-prints near the garden;
bucks restlessly polished their racks
against the bent Locust.

Evening came, clouded the sky
with a metallic gray,
veiled May's full moon,
unleashed spirited tides
that pulled like Heracles' winged horse.

Thunder cramped! Lightening slashed!
The wind panted to the rhythm of your birthing.
The beat of rain blended with your sturdy cry.
Nature attended to your nativity.

Colic

From the moment of birth
you cried in protest
as if the lights were too bright
sounds too stark
movements too sharp
air too chilled
as if rushed from the womb
without your approval.

Weeks later you still arch
your back, clench your fists
and cry until you're crimson
as if demanding to go back
to that muted world where
waves lapped to the rhythm
of intimate heartbeats.

But the two who waited
yearn to comfort and engage you.
Soon you will detect your mother's
smile as it rises in her eyes
and recognize the silk of her hair
as it catches in your searching fingers.

The First Pressing

You will know your father's bearded
cheek as he presses his face to yours
and you will sleep easily
within the sling of his arm.

Deer Domain

As I wash the window
from inside,
I watch you
prodigally spend your way
through my yard.
You strip the arbor vita
as high as your teeth can reach,
mooch the dark green
of the lilac,
loot the tulips as they awaken.
When you lope toward the heart
of my Gold Dust hosta,
I want to rap on the glass
and stop you
from filching my garden trophy!
But, oh, the swagger
of your penny-colored back
the swing of your tawny neck
the flip of your white tail
your princely stance
remind me
that this was your dominion first
and I am the trespasser.

*Putti

*Italian for Cupid-like children
in Italian sculpture; angels, cherubs

Some babies were ferried
in the solid sure beak of a stork.
Others—like Thumbelina—grew
out of the center of a red and yellow tulip.
Before his lively transformation,
Pinocchio was a common block of firewood.
Stories abound of quaint beginnings.
Even Moses was discovered floating
in a reed basket among the bull rushes.
But you were so beloved that Putti,
with their roseate smiles,
their harps and wings, flew
with you to your swaying cradle.

First Communion

I see the small bread dropped in the small hand
fingers reaching to take and eat.
Blond head bowed, family circled around
I see the small bread in the small hand.
Communion of saints, earth and beyond,
my children, their children, sacral rite repeats.
I see the small bread in the small hand
fingers poised, she takes and eats.

Windchimes

On my porch I am
embracing the sun—

These windchimes are
subdued bells of a distant
church;

These bees
genuflect
on rows of potted marigolds—

The breeze pushes through trees.

Birds leave their branches;
journey; dip; drink;
wash in ritual ablution.

Donna Wahlert

I meditate:

I ask the creator of that searing sun
to energize me;
I ask that the sound of my life
echo
ethereal as windchimes,
harmonious as the song
echoing from the church
beyond—

I ask that I will be cleansed
and refreshed and empowered—
a pilgrim of the earth;

I ask that I find
the elusive nectar
in a cache both as hidden and obvious
as the sweetness
in the dependable marigold.

Part Two

Summer

"you…taste a pearl moon shell, rattle a sand dollar"

We Have Moved To A New House

We have moved
to a new house
half the equator
away from the old.
Pin oaks, poplars,
maples that turn
colors like chameleons
are replaced
by the eternal green
of royal palms,
queen palms, black
olives, xanadu.

The juniper and arbor vita
are adding their inches
without me. The cardinals
and chickadees are fed
by someone else.
Here we trim the Japonicum,
India Hawthorne, Shell Ginger;
watch the Fakahatchee grass
swirl in a gulf coast breeze.

The First Pressing

Everything feels strange
—like trying on
someone else's wedding
ring or sleeping
on your spouse's side of the bed.
The house is empty
and the ten foot ceilings yell back
our words and the glazed
tile floors bounce
around loud footprints
and the scuff of each chair.

With curtain-less windows
and walls of sliding glass,
neighbors watch me trying
to tame this house
like a large stubborn dog.
But I have rationed
out rewards of beef jerky
have practiced with authority
commands to "sit, stay, heel;"
have bent to praise and nuzzle.
Now the aloofness, the wariness
has given way.

Donna Wahlert

Rugs have softened
the harsh foot falls,
draperies dredge up
our words like flour on a cutlet,
sofas add gracious curves.
The four-poster bed
with the soufflé-high mattress
that would protect a princess
from the tiniest pea
is comfortable in its new space.

The mother-and-child
painting has been hung.
My finger has moved
every candle and bookend
and picture frame
to its exactness.
The house and I
breathe together now
like an old couple
reading the morning paper
over strong coffee.

A Three-Year-Old Visits

We saunter over to the tomato vines—
bracketed by thin poles—and I advise
"Just pick the ripe ones."
What does "ripe" mean, you ask?

In my lengthening shadow
I want to define it as:
nodding to the future,

mature, bold, mellow,
like apples edging toward cider
like the ruby grape ready for pressing.

But I say, "Ripe means perfect,
sweet, red, ready, just right,
like the age of three; like you
visiting me in my garden."

Climbing Down the Rocky Mountains

I climb down the Rocky mountains
rock down the climby mountains
pass through five foot ferns
pass by four foot fawns
ferns fanning
fawns feigning
famed ferns
finest fawns

I slide down the stony ledges
to Queen Ann's lace and tiny sunflowers
slide stones down the sludgy edges
the queen sunning
lacing the sedges
the tiniest queen
laciest sun
ferns framing
fawns facing

The First Pressing

I sprint down the lower mountain
Lower the slant of dawning
to star-shaped columbine and purple lupine
lace the purples
crown the lupine
loop the star-crossed
shape the mountain
ferns fluming
fawns flicking

I careen down to the bedrock of the mountain
rock the bed of the careening mountain
greet whistling aspen
bustle past creeping thistle
aspens waving
thistle tasseling
ferns fasting
fawns fading
the mountain lasting.

Flora

Flora,
The Roman goddess of flowers
Shares your name!
Like her
You are leaf lovely
Petal perfect
Firmly rooted
Grounded
Upright.

No pesky weeds
Thorny thistles
Slippery snails
Nor translucent beetles
Can mar your bloom.

Flora, your namesake,
With sculpted wreath
And ample body,
Will depart her temple
Will disappear from Latin coins

The First Pressing

And come to guard you—
*Nova puella, filia, amica
of the Roman goddess of flowers.

*In Latin: new little girl, daughter, friend

Music to My Ears

When your baby mouth
formed your first word
for "Grama," I heard a chorus
of tiny Suzuki violins.

When you were old enough
to talk to me on the telephone,
it was flute notes bouncing along
the wires from Minnesota to Iowa.

You began taking music lessons,
then spoke to me in piano tones:
brisk scales, nimble arpeggios
rapt chords, four sharps.

Now your words ring out in cyberspace
like sounds of clapping cymbals
as you tap out your message: "Grama,
I have my own e-mail address now."

Separation

Scripture says that
the woman with child

sorrows as her time
to be delivered dawns.

Implied is fear of cramping,
pushing, gaping pain.

I've panted and groaned through that
a handful of times.

It's real. It's frightening.
It's forgotten.

The pain that lingers is the salty sting
of separation.

For nine months, Gospel woman and I
are all our child wants and needs.

We are food, cradle, armor,
his entire universe.

Donna Wahlert

He is our work and gift,
mission and creation.

To propel him
into a world that forgets

to nurture and shelter and cherish
claws out in us a throbbing hollowness.

Years later that stinging cycle repeats.
Muscled, tall, and bold,

the child sheds his womb of home.
Charting maps,

cramming cartons,
tying shut hatchback lid,

he crowds his future into
a compact car.

Expectantly
he waves as he drives

out of the zone of security
into a world that worries

about its destiny.
This separation,

The First Pressing

as inevitable and prophesied as the first,
chisels out its own aching hollowness.

Meditation at 7:00 a.m.

I turn towards the woods behind me.
The sun breaks through sapling oaks,
the dense poplar, the lacy arbor vita,
like the flame of a candle in a storm-dark room,
like the sanctuary lamp in a silent monastery,
like God emerging through a dark tunnel of doubt.

Generations

We time the dull stabs of your first labor
Your womb a ripened plum,
mine a dusty fig
> aches to have you back
> in its dark spicy center
> safe

Mine would do the pulsing and cramping
Mine would do the pushing
that sends you
> both forth
> like carved Russian dolls
> un-nesting

But I cannot hold you in my branches and shade you
cannot strip away like bark
> the pain
> that grooves this memory into you
> like the rings of a tree.

The Transplant

I planted purple impatiens
on the crescent of my yard.
I placed them eight inches
apart—as I would up north—
hoping they would overspread,
leaf touching leaf
petal edging purple petal.

I dug shallow holes in the thin
layer of potting soil spread
across the Florida sand.
I tamped, watered and prepared
to wait a month—maybe more.
Within two weeks, mature
flowers and new buds filled
the spaces, the gaps of earth.

Now in a different
climate, a new seed bed,
my own transplanting
parallels my purple plants.

The First Pressing

What I thought would be months
of lonely spaces and unfilled gaps
filled quickly. I found new neighbors
criss-crossing the street like a sandal strap
with strudel, cheese cake, lasagna,
an Allen wrench, a Phillips, a bicycle rack.

I discovered new places: sloughs and preserves
with slash pines, duck weed and broom sedge;
anhingas drying their cape-like wings
alligators sunning on the rim of the pond
palm trees shedding their lower fronds.

I feel like lichen slowly growing
on a cypress, a swamp iris finding
its place among palmettos.
I have stretched like my seedlings.
I feel as solid as earth, as young as water,
as natural as purple petal beside purple petal.

God As Heat

The warmth of you
is in the summer wind,
in the sun's red
and the moon's gold.

Your heat radiates
like August on hot sand
and on the rock ridges
of bluff tops.

I look for you
in the phantom pools,
shimmering waves
rising from the road.

Your energy hovers
like a humming bird;
friction of wings,
movement imperceptible.

Ballooning Over Minnesota

They balloon over Minnesota
float over new-born lakes
rise toward the hidden moon
loons crooning
minnows playing
trout yawning
otters preening.

Hot air leaking, altitude needing
they fire up, burner flashing
sail across marshy fields
wild rice waving
marsh grass weaving
sun flowers fielding
burners sighing.

They hover over muscled oaks
skim the steeples of slender pines
catch the stride of white-tailed deer
acorns hardening
pine cones steeping
saplings swooning
deer stretching.

Donna Wahlert

They follow the shore of Lake Superior
cliffs of granite
rock shingle beaches
waves falling
waterfalls slipping
clouds diluting
sky expanding.

They move along, descend slowly,
basket creaking
breezes steering
the red fox stirring
creeks basking
steers grazing
the earth slowing.

Making Way For the Interstate

For several days he passes the Victorian house
where the wrecking machine stands
glaring at pillars and balcony
with its eye-like bolt.
Then one gray morning it swings
and slams its long arm
into a family's history.

The turn-of-the-century house
slides down on its knees
as if pleading to end the execution quickly.
For weeks the State has slowly stripped
it of copper gutters,
robbed it of oaken doors,
pried off woodwork of mellowed mahogany.

Now the jaws of the yellow dragon
bite into pipes and wire
and brick that once
were fused into a dream.
Dirt and bits of cement slip
through its teeth as it repeatedly
spits out a mouthful into an idling truck.

Donna Wahlert

Men in hard hats signal "thumbs up"
at their progress swift and clean.
Nothing remains
but the crater
that held root cellar and coal bin.
A chill emptiness seeps from the hole;
the dust hovers like spirits displaced.

Concerning Dogs

While traveling through England,
we found these signs posted regarding dogs:

Dogs Are Welcome!

*Guests kindly ensure that your pet dogs
do not soil the bed and chair covers.*

*Sorry, dogs may not be brought
into public rooms where food is served.*

*Please attempt to keep your dogs
from fouling the park.*

Dogs Are Welcome!

While driving through the United States,
we found these signs regarding dogs:

Donna Wahlert

NO DOGS ALLOWED!
KEEP DOGS LEASHED AND MUZZLED
BEWARE OF DOG!
GUARD DOG ON DUTY!
THIS AREA PATROLLED BY DOGS!

Is there a correlation between the civility
of a nation and how it treats its dogs?

Evening Drama

Dusk lowers its scrim.
Fireflies become
winking footlights.

Storm Signals

Lower back aches;
neck stiffens;
crooked fingers throb.
Soon a summer storm.

In The Garden With My Grandson

On this hot humid Iowa summer day,
we water seven clay pots of flowers,
pick off the spent geraniums,

mist the basil, pull meddlesome weeds,
check the ripening cherry tomatoes.
He fills the bird feeder to the brim

with safflower and thistle seed.
Taking up his own perch, he watches
quietly and detects birds that are rarely here:

the purple finch, downy woodpecker,
warbler, waxwing, golden crowned kinglet.
In hospitality, he fills the birdbath

with cool clean water overflowing.
Witnessing his vigilance and care,
I too, am filled to the brim, to overflowing.

This Mississippi

This river—this Mississippi
has become a part of me.
It flows in me as steadily
as it moves within its river banks.
It has seeped into my cells
as it does the sand on its beaches.
Past the shallows of its edges
I step into its rich muddy bottom
down inside me somewhere.
Its bluffs line my interior landscape
the rock walls fortressing me.
Its constant current sweeps me
to fresh inlets, undiscovered islands.
Just as the water that arrives each day is new
I wade into a curl that has never been there before
and I am swept away on an ever-changing journey.

An Astonishing Side Trip

Traveling through Cornwall, near Land's End,
we took a side road winding to the sea.
Rising up from the edge of the white cliffs
was a remarkable stone amphitheater.
Sitting on smoothed rocks, wrapped
in plaid woolen rugs, and surrounded
by Mark & Spencer hampers,
the British were eating smoked turkey
and spooning Trifle onto Royal Doulton plates.
As they awaited the curtain's rising on *Jane Eyre*,
they sipped champagne from Waterford flutes
and toasted Bronte and the sea
as it clapped against the stone stage.

"And then on every table in the world, salt…"
Ode to Salt
Pablo Neruda

Ode to Bread

On every table in the world is bread. Shape-changing like a wizard, loaves are round, oval, square as a thatched-roofed cottage in the Cotswolds; twisted into Jewish challah like a grandmother's thick silver braid; or worn with the topknot of a brioche, a Parisian chignon; or even a stalk of baguette carried like the gendarme's baton.

Bread can be soft on the inside like batting from a sofa cushion; crusty on the outside, a crab shell; or both—like men posturing with their sons. It can be hollow, a pita waiting for a surprise; a flat scoop for Lebanese tabuli; or curved to cradle beans and chilies. Bread can be as heavy as a Welsh mist, as light as a day on the beach at Portofino; but as it bakes, its aroma rises like a mystic's levitating body.

Romanesque hands, stubby fingers, gnarled knuckles, callused palms stained with mechanic's grease, fists of small children—all grasp the bread. Bread is on the table. Shape-changing. On every table in the world is bread.

Wedding Cake

She found work in a steamy bakery
her sixteenth summer,
iced doughnuts with the chocolate
blade of her hand,
stuffed crullers onto spigots
filled with jelly,
sealed crusty baguettes
into slippery cellophane.

Next summer she was elevated
to a stiffly starched uniform
and selling pastries on the cooled retail side.
She kept trays brimming
in the lighted glass cases,
plucked the cash register of brocaded bronze.
A worthy subject, she was crowned
with pleated tiara,

anointed as the keeper
of the "Wedding Cake Book."
She learned about sugar scrolls,
butter cream roses,
icing patterns that resembled
eyelet and dotted swiss.

The First Pressing

She spoke regally of bells and fans
and miniature couples

that ruled over towering tiers.
She described delicacy
of flavor and airiness of texture
to mothers and betrothed daughters
whose eyes sparkled like their rings.
She escorted them through the album
of nuptial confections,
pausing as they praised

the columned "Romanesque,"
the gilded "Versailles,"
the minarets of "Marrakech."
They chatted about beaded bodices,
sweeping cathedral trains,
stephanotis, freesia and the harpist's glissades.
They and a thousand others
have ordered their fantasy

from her majestic book of cakes.
Now with hair as white as her pleated laurel,
she is known as the queen-mother of weddings.
The brides have become her royal daughters
though she has had no ring
nor cake
of her
own.

East meets West

Today is my birthday.
I am packing for a trip to China.
On our agenda is Shanghai
where relics of the Ming Dynasty
stand next to modern skyscrapers,
where east meets west in harmony.

We'll move on to Beijing, The Great Wall,
the Summer Palace,
the Forbidden City with its golden tiled roofs,
the expanses of Tiananmen Square,
the haunting memories of Tiananmen Square
where the young were cut down
by the old regime,
where the young were cheated
of their golden birthdays.

My friend brings birthday flowers
to my front door; among them are Columbine
with red blooms from the eastern states
and blue from the Rocky Mountains.
Here again, east meets west.

The First Pressing

I think of Colorado's Columbine
dripping in red
where the young were cut down
by the young;
where many will never have
another golden summer.

I am allowed a birthday wish today.
I will blow out my candles and wish away
the great walls of violence.
I will wish our young people
—both east and west—
palaces and skyscrapers of peace,
new springs, summers of justice,
undying harmony, flowers for their birthdays.

Nine-Eleven

Written on 10/11

As someone raised in Iowa on nursery rhymes and fairy tales in a town where the tallest thing on the corn-fed landscape was the local Cathedral, I thought of New York's twin towers as two massive bean stalks climbing up to the giant beyond the skyline.

Then one day while standing in my bedroom watching the morning news, I saw the stalks crumble as if the giant stomped on them with two large airborne shoes. Exploding, imploding upon himself, the giant pulled the stalks down, taking with him all the Jacks and all the Jills that came tumbling after.

The flames, the thick sooty smoke, the crumbling steel, the acres of burnt Holocaust played, re-winded, played, re-winded again and again in my mind. So many were lost; so much was lost.

I wondered if the golden goose, who had given so much to America, lie dead in the rubble too.

The First Pressing

Those not ready to give up fairy tales may see the golden goose skimming across the nation as shadows of the protective fighter planes, shading us with the safety of their wings as if we were goslings.

Others may feel that there is no place for nursery rhymes and fairy tale endings any more. But I remind myself that we still have a nest of golden eggs: our four freedoms as painted by Norman Rockwell; the anthem describing "The land of the free and the home of the brave," penned by Francis Scott Key in the flare of erupting battle; the Spirit of the Lady who lights the way with her torch for the tired, the poor, the huddled masses.

As the fires still smolder and smoke rises from the twisted whitened steel, it is almost like incense rising from an altar. It is like the image of the tall lonely Cathedral that I have seen on the Iowa landscape. This is a new icon. This is Holy Space

"Day comes, and the brightness is hidden around me."
Enheduanna, high priestess, 2300 B.C.E.
<u>Women in Praise of the Sacred</u>, Jane Hirshfield

Nocturne

O God, there you are, revealed again
in a star hidden in the luster of day.
In the sun, I fumbled for you, my Talisman.
O God, there you are, revealed again;
you encircle me like the invisible meridian.
Only in dark night does the lodestar glister on clay.
O God, there you are! Revealed again,
you are a star hidden in the veil of day.

Part Three

Autumn

"The red fruit is at its peak
these moments too, are ripe and full, ready for gathering"

Another Season

Part 1

His small hand
grips
his father's
index finger
as they follow
the blurred path
between unruly
orchard trees.
Tin pail
in hand,
the father
talks
apple picking;
his thoughts
go deeper
like the roots
of these trees.
The red fruit
is at its peak.

The First Pressing

These moments too
are ripe
and full,
ready
for gathering.

Part 2
Two years later

Windfall in the Orchard

The four year old
swings
his wicker basket;
the younger sister
spurts
down the path.
The father clasps
a hand of each
and leads them
to the trees
heavy with fruit.
Exploring
the orchard,
they will learn more
than just apples today.
They will taste
the sweetness
of red,
pucker the tartness
of green.

The First Pressing

They will notice
the windfalls
on the ground
already turning
back to the soil.

They will discover
that for everything
on earth
there is
a perfect moment.

Animal Blessing for the Feast of St. Francis of Assisi

O God, source of all life and energy,
You who created the animals because your universe
was incomplete without them,
bless these loving creatures that we bring
before You today.
Bless these cats and dogs and mammals
who amble through your grasses.
Bless these birds that wing the rich air
that You breathe forth.
Bless these fish that dart through
the living waters that You provide
and these snakes that slither with a kind agenda.
Protect all of them from harm
and their own curiosities.
Bless the caretakers of these animal companions.
Nourish them so that they may reflect the simplicity,
honesty, and unconditional love of these pets.
Mindful of your desire for harmony and wholeness
within all of your creation, and inspired by St. Francis,
we ask these things with humble faith.

Observing Thanksgiving

One part lard, three parts flour,
the ball of dough sits on the floured board.
It will be rolled, patted into a pie tin,
pinched and thumbed into a fluted
ring that will hold the pumpkin
filling like a golden brown crown.

She creams butter and honey-colored
sugar, whips the eggs and milk,
gently folds in pumpkin pureed,
anoints with the sacred spices:
cinnamon, mace, hand-grated
nutmeg, a fleck of ancient sea salt.

The recipe, handed down to her
by her mother, the housekeeper
of a stately Missouri mansion,
calls for a few jiggers of bourbon.
She splashes it in, tastes, pours, bakes.
If wine can become an altar sacrament,
a grail of bourbon in a pumpkin pie
can mark the holiness of the harvest.

The Quilters

The cluster of friends
sits in a circle
like quilters piecing
and tying together
each of their stories.

One re-threads her sorrow
for her stillborn son.
Another cuts and shapes
the thirty-nine days
of her daughter's brief life.
Still another stitches in the pain
of losing a grandchild.

Then one examines
her own stained satin square
—tucked away for ten years now—
of a baby who was becoming.
She strokes the patch with her hand
holds it against her cheek.
The grief is as near as her breath.
Slowly
She offers it to the circle of quilters.

Sonnet To My Daughter
on Her Twenty-First Birthday

Fall is the sweet and crisp season of your birth.
This Autumn holds a promise in her titian hues
Of a new stage of life ripely springing forth
When maturity and wisdom will color your views.
We tried to prepare you for this growing venture:
Grooming you through schooling, rooting you in faith,
Seeking to balance love and mild censure,
Nurturing your spirit, keeping visions safe.
Now you have come of age, toasted twenty-one,
Proved prudent with a budget and lived away from home,
In-gathered friends who share their shafts of sun.
You are ready to emerge, shed childhood's sheltered womb.
Embrace and explore with elfin Lady Autumn,
Then reap and prune for yet another season.

I Wish I could Write a Poem About My Mother

I am so full of her.

I pass
a mirror
and glimpse her
sugar-white hair,
her M o d i g l i a n i curved neck.

I glance down
and recognize
her spare bosom
ample hip-line
and AAA narrow feet.

I speak
and hear
her love of words:
the droll adjective
turn-of-the-century verb.

The First Pressing

I laugh
and hear
the Midwestern
modesty
of her chuckle.

I touch
my arm
and know we have both
left tautness
to the next generation.

I catch
a scent
upon my skin
and know
it was hers first.

My Grandmother's Kitchen

When I think of my grandmother's kitchen, I am
surrounded by white. White wooden cupboards
with hutch tops and a roll-top bread box; pearl-white
slightly chipped porcelain counters; ivory wallpaper
spritzed with a frosted pattern; bleached linoleum
faded from the sun; a massive kitchen table covered
with chalky oil cloth and perched on thick white
legs—much like her own that were always covered
with beige lisle stockings rolled down below the
kneecap with strangulating garters.

My grandmother dusted the kitchen with a haze of
flour as she scooped up handfuls for piecrusts,
noodles, dumplings—the only measuring tool her
cupped fingers.

A light oak icebox held local farm eggs and sturdy
glass bottles of milk with an inch of cream at the
neck. The wood stove hummed with broth boiling.
The propane oven vented aromas of yeast rising,
apple slices bubbling with cinnamon.

The First Pressing

When days are dim or times darken, I float back to that white kitchen, feel cool porcelain, hear Irish songs lifting, imagine floury hands and thick cotton stockings.

Blessing For Family Reunion

O God, Creator of this delicate universe,
Designer of this tender society called family,
be with us tonight as we welcome our cousins
into our home for this reunion dinner.

You have blest this family in so many ways.
You have laughed with us in our joys,
and carried us through our sorrows.
Grace us as we gather now and in the coming year.

Give us peace and tranquility;
let us put aside all anxieties.
Let us recognize the gifts and graces that
have been poured so generously upon us.

Bless this food that has been prepared with love
and attention and from recipes of generations past.
In our bounty, let us remember those who
do not have family or who have too little to eat.

Assemble all our relatives who are with you already,
especially our parents and grandparents
and all our loved ones, so they may celebrate
at Your banquet and join us in Spirit tonight.

*Novena

On *Taking care of my daughter after the birth of her child*
**(A Novena is a series of nine prayers)*

Grilled steak, pink and on the bias
Chicken draped with honey sauce
Streusel muffins popping with apple bits
Cheesecake levitating above cashew crust

Sun-bleached laundry in smooth stacks
Beds bosomed with fresh pillows
Miles of newly laid carpet sweeper tracks
Bathroom chrome winking like an understudy
A kitchen wiped down like the galley of a Norse ship

I wrap these things like Tiffany gifts
and offer them to you as prayers.

Dust

As a child I left it behind me
    like a cat with powdered paws.
        In college I hovered above it with Plato
        as it gathered in my dorm
        like tumbleweed.

As a young mother
    with a shoe full of children
        laced into a world
        of pot roasts and track meets
        time was scarce to chase it down
            with thinned diapers.

Now alone with my
    bronzed memories
        it still seeps in under my door
        sifts through window screens
        spins pollen webs in serene corners.

The First Pressing

Dust could give me an agenda
    for the entire day;
        but I prefer to buff a few bars of grace notes
        hand-scrub a strophe of poetry
        chamois a still-life
            —before I too
            become a layer of it.

Old Loves Revisited

She sits on the beach
and watches honeyed couples
cling across the sand.

Her hair like silvered sea oats now,
she gazes at the sun
spins visions of her old loves.

The first flew off like Icarus
to live above the clouds
piloting jet planes.

The next melted
into liquid columns of figures
in his accounting ledger.

The engineer built himself a
bridge to Canada when she told him
she couldn't see them together on the horizon.

The last ran over her heart
with his Volkswagen Beetle
and his singular shyness.

The First Pressing

She turns to him now
on their shell-anchored blanket;
he pats her sandy knee.
Thirty years of waves have washed
his shyness into quiet fidelity.

Go Figure...

Inspired by Anna Akhmatova's poem
"He loved Three Things."

He brought with him:
    a library on World War II
    three generations of management
    a Volkswagen Beetle
    a dented trumpet
    and his own silver napkin ring.

She brought with her:
    Frayed books of poetry
    jitter-bug lessons
    a box of recipes with butter thumbprints
    a blessing of fertility and short labors
    and a legacy of grandfathers who kept their hair.

...And they have been married for 40 years.

Last Chance

She was slim with alabaster skin
& salt & pepper hair in a Gibson Girl
pompadour & she wore linen suits & starched
shirtwaists & a face that the sun had never
brushed (cleansed only with a pad of witch
hazel.) Unmarried, she lived with her brother &
his wife & entertained a gentleman farmer in the
kitchen with his own gift of hand-cranked
ice cream.

It was improper to show him through
to her rooms with brocade settee, Italian
marble-topped bureau with attached jewelry box
& the silver scrolled mirror, brush & comb,
the commode with gilt-edged wash basin
& delicate chamber pot covered with an
embroidered lid, hidden inside the cupboard door.

Donna Wahlert

Theirs was a long and proper courtship.
But gradually she had become fearful of leaving
the house & so always relegated to kitchen
& custard, the farmer stopped coming & more
gray crept into her hair that now lay in a thick
braid down the back of her wrap-around house
dress & oxfords replaced chic black patent
pumps & the color on her high cheek bones
faded.

She began to collect newspapers, brown grocery
bags, thin strands of meat string & she never
threw away a canceled stamp, rubber band,
scrap of tinfoil or cellophane & piles of discards
covered her settee, the bureau, the commode &
the worn rug covering the cold floor & her still
unlined face was ashen & her hair—yellowed,
loose and long—touched by age and oil & she
wore only a bulky woolen bathrobe & carpet
slippers slit on the sides to accommodate her
bunions & for her remaining years she paced the
narrow path that led to her bed.

"I come from a house with no floors."
Quote from an unknown student at a poetry workshop.
Intrigued by this, I wrote a poem around this mysterious person.

I come from a house with no floors.

At times she thought there were solid floors & then her legs would crash through a second story & her hips would be encased in ceiling plaster like a Charlie Chaplin stunt & at other times, the floor would suddenly open like a trap door on a stage & she would fall swiftly, hitting some hard cold surface with the soles of her feet, pain ricocheting up through her ankles, up the legs past the shin splints, through the damaged knee cartilage, stinging through the thighs, crashing along the pelvis, along the whole spinal cord to the cervical discs to the back of the brain where pain would splinter into points of light like fireworks breaking open a dark Fourth of July.

She learned to walk gingerly along the edges, avoiding the center where there was nothing to hold onto like a windowsill, curtain hem, picture hook, telephone cord & she learned to be comforted by cool plaster walls & the transparency of window panes, reading her life by Braille along the perimeter.

Donna Wahlert

It was maybe forty years before she could send
down her own shoot through that floorless house,
past the second story & the first, beyond the
basement, down down like a cactus searching out
water & finally find a mound of earth friendly to her
slim stem, allowing it to root, centering it to grow
straight, to send out new leaves, to bud, to flower.
She is still tempted at times to listen for the squeak
in the plank, test for dry rot, watch for carpenter
ants, but she can cross wide expanses now without
looking down.

To A Lost Grandmother

You were gone before I was born
faded from photographs
snipped out of conversations
your French soul—a hole.

You never held me.

We never made jam
sipped tea with citron
pinched back the wisteria vine.

Now, at my midpoint
you linger in my space
like the secret sound of a deer
that has lately passed by.

I feel your cells in my cells
your thin bone in my bone
Even the aura of your hair
reflects in my mirror.

Donna Wahlert

And I grieve to know:

Who sat with you as your life cooled?
Did someone catch your last light breath
before it folded into all the deaths
of all our grandmothers
who passed too soon?

A Catholic Woman Asks:
Who is Priest?

They wear robes sashed at the waist
Cradle new-borns for their first immersion
Instruct children about the life within
Quietly listen, gently counsel those in pain
Forgive those who have fallen
Guide those promised in marriage
Cleanse and comfort the dying
And always prepare the bread
And wash the cup.

These are honored as charisms
Of a priest;
But since the time of Eve
They have been the daily sacraments
Of woman.

Yet she is forbidden to bring these gifts
To the altar
Or minister in robe and Roman collar
Or hope for the holy chrism of Ordination :
She who was anointed to carry
Christ in her womb.

Still Life

We have stretched past
our middle years, olive trees
ready for the late autumn pressing.

Our children are grown, ripe as Bosc pears.
Our grandchildren are in the vineyard
awaiting their first cutting.

Our fathers are asleep in the field.
Our mothers walk in the mist
toward the furrows.

Some of our leaves have faded;
some pile up on dried grasses.
But we still have patches

of cobalt green and yellow ochre
layered on us with a kind palette knife.
The light still comes from the east.

We gently await
the artist's next brush stroke;
savoring this stolen season.

Part Four

Winter

"I, a snowy owl on a snowy fencepost,
dream of soaring with you."

Snowbirds

Twice a year, we drive 1500 miles
to a new climate, to a new season.
Southbound, we travel from Midwestern
hills and rocky river cliffs
to subtropic sand and salted sea air;
from a thick brick house to a stucco house;
from old friends to newer friends just as dear
as those we are leaving.

Like snowbirds, we *could* fly.
The trip would be three days shorter.
We could go instantly from cool damp fall nights
to the balmy breezes of palm fronds;
from walking in crisp leaves under brisk skies
to walking bare foot on beaches
under infinite blueness.

But we *need* that trio of days
to slow down the process of red maples
and oaks melting into moss-hung
live oaks, scrub pines, queen palms.
Cross a few state lines
and sumac and dried corn stalks
change to cotton, kudzu, palmettos, broom sedge.

The First Pressing

Trees heavy with apples flow into peach trees,
then rough bark trunks
with a canopy of smooth pecans,
then finally spicy aromatic orange groves.

Winding our way through lines
of both longitude and latitude,
we enter enduring heat, endless sunshine
and the briny atmosphere at sea level.
Like the scuba diver, we need a lapse of time
to decompress our parting
and our coming home;
our coming home
and our parting.

On Folding Napkins For a Dinner Party

With my thumb, I crease a two-inch hem
on the rim of a napkin,
then easily roll it into a Roman Candle.
Experimenting with different shapes,
I refold the linen square
and form the three exact points
of a Fleur-de-Lis. With two more steps,
it changes into a proper Bishop's Mitre.
I fold again, and with difficulty, create
a tiny Lady's Slipper, then unwrap it instantly.
It resembles too much a woman's bound foot.

This flow of diverse napkin forms
strikes me as a symbol for our generation.
The pattern in childhood was fluid, easily shaped.
Then the 1950's ushered in sharply
creased rules of etiquette, stiff girdles,
white gloves, prim hats with veils;
tightly woven fiats from church and state;
the culture's starched and limited
expectations for girls.

The First Pressing

It has taken half a century
to unpin those veils,
shed the gloves,
loosen threads, shake out the fabric,
stamp a tiny foot against limitations.
Gliding into our sixties, we have given up
the formality of the Fleur-de-Lis,
the sharp stringent lines of the Bishop's Mitre,
the confined image of the Lady Slipper.
We definitely choose to begin and end
our lives with Roman Candles.

When the Time Comes

When the time comes,
I want a nursing home room
with a private bath
and personal computer.
I want my MAC along side my rocker,
a laser printer on my bureau,
poem fragments on my night stand—
along with my teeth and my laxative.

Strands

Your eyes
snapping
brown,
your skin
summery
smooth;
my eyes
fading
to green,
skin creeping
to sheerness;
your hair
slick black,
mine careening
to whiteness;
Our lives
are woven
together
like a braid,
wrapping round
nesting into
one another.

Donna Wahlert

You
a chickadee,
touching down
for only
a moment,

I
a snowy owl
on a snowy fencepost
dream of soaring
with you.

The Jelly Maker

Massaging the thinning bone
of her hip, she sways at the stove
while heat and fruity vapors
circle her like her dance partner
of fifty-nine years.
Her opal-pale hands pluck
strands of glossy berries,
dropping them into a spackled

enameled vat, adding
"just enough" water
from a tarnished copper kettle.
The currants cook up to a boil,
simmer down to a ruby juice
that pours like the last
of his elderberry wine
into the stained cotton jelly bag.

Donna Wahlert

When the last red drops
drip into the crock below,
she sweetens, adds pectin,
shuffles the syrup onto the flame
stirring, stirring, testing
until the clotting elixir
sheets off the metal spoon.

Bent now like the currant bough
she inserts a dented funnel
into jars once emptied by their sons.
She transfuses the glasses
with scarlet gel,
seals each with the fevery wax
that cools into a thick white cap—
preserving this last gleaning
for the deepening winter season.

Lucy Conquers ALS

I slip into your hospice room
for my final good-bye.
Your body, hours from death,
your mind, sharp as a blade,
you comfort me as I lean over you.
Patting my back with your frail arm,
you smile and whisper, "friend."
I sense another soul present in the room
as your eyes suddenly become translucent
with peace and joy.
I ask if it is your husband,
whose life was cut short just last year.
You nod, smile, and are swept
into unspoken conversation,
silent agreements with him.
I retreat from the room, understanding
that soon he will fly with you past the planets,
sail with you to the corners of the universe,
breeze with you through the lobby of paradise.

Leningrad of January, 1986

The Curtain Falls

Leningrad in January is:
piercing dampness
piles of dingy snow
frozen chips of peeling paint
cold threadbare hotels.
Even our bones wear hoarfrost.

With surprise tickets to the Kirov
for a ballet set to the poetry of Mayakovsky,
we hope for ageless Russian themes
finely nuanced characters
drama wrapped around us like eider down.

Instead the stage is drowned
in red silk
the blood of the Revolution;
the evening is chilled by dogmatic monologues
and red flags flapping propaganda.

The First Pressing

The ghost of Mother Russia
is only unearthed
by the classic ballet
who's soul is rooted
deeper than Marxist bromides.

The curtain falls.

The audience sits—coolly
taps finger tips together
for the poetry of boots and banners;
but rises
with heavy thumping hands
and Slavic shouts of affection
for the bowing ballerina—
Russian icon and legacy.

"Perestroika" and "glasnost"
are still in the throat
have not yet passed warm lips;
but we feel a drawing of new breath
in this audience, in this Leningrad.

In China During Christmas

In China, there is no Christmas.
There is no recognition of December twenty-fifth.
It is a regular workday, a normal school day.
No one spends weeks selecting just the right gift
for someone; no one gives gifts.
You do not tip the mail carrier,
the deliverer of your newspaper,
the person who, rain or snow, collects your trash.
There are no pine trees shimmering with colorful

lights, raining with tinsel, crowned by an angel.
There is no manger scene below it.
The father and mother with child are unknown.
The wise men with exotic names remain anonymous—
their presence and their gifts not understood.
There are no gingerbread men baking
their spices into the kitchen,
no eggnog and rum standing by for a guest
who may drop in.

There is no Christmas turkey or goose
turning golden brown.
No carols are heard. No "Silent Night,"
No "O Come All Ye faithful," no "Jingle Bells."

The First Pressing

In fact, there are no bells. Nothing is tinkling,
not even the steady rhythm of the Salvation
Army bell outside a market.
In China, there are many holidays,
but no Christmas.

If your work takes you abroad to live in China
you must pack up an artificial tree,
a collection of ornaments,
your shepherds and sheep and manger figurines.
The recipes for favorite Christmas cookies
must be collected; you must slip in a book of carols
and the recordings that inspire you each year.
In China, or someplace else where December
twenty-fifth is just another day,

You must carry Christmas with you.
You must reflect the beauty of the tree,
the love of the family by the manger,
the significance of the carols,
the hospitality of aromatic sweets
and the warmth of eggnog with rum.
You must unfold the meaning
and spirit of Christmas
and elevate it above "just another day."

Gabriel

I am Gabriel, trusted Messenger from God.
I have announced, guided and instructed
God's chosen ones for millennia.

I have always had certitude about my mission.
I remain calm, serene, and easily pick the perfect moment.
But tonight I shake and quake and flutter

with the significance of my message
to a hand maiden from Nazareth, a virgin,
not yet twenty years, a lowly handmaid from a lowly country.

I must tell her that she will bear the Son of the Most High,
that He will reign over the house of Jacob
that His kingdom will have no end.

She will be stunned at my very visit.
She is so humble that she will find it difficult
to believe that she has found favor with God.

How will I ever begin to explain that she will be over-shadowed
by the Holy Spirit and will bring forth a son,
the perfect Man, the Savior of all time?

The First Pressing

What if I garble the message? What if she says, "No"?
I must stop this pacing, this rehearsing, this jumping
to conclusions. The moment is almost here.

I must resume the grace of my angel ways,
plunge to earth, and face this greatest
moment in my eternal life.
I am Gabriel, trusted Messenger of God.

Closing In

For almost eighty years my father hid his secret;
    packed it away
in a dark cabinet, never to be handed down like
    family crystal.
After a stroke shattered his speech, imprisoning
    him between the floors
of the voiceless, a nurse whispered to me that
    he was acutely claustrophobic.
Her truth splintered in my hand, shards of glass
    reflecting up
my own fears of sealed space, years of muffled
    struggle.
Windowless rooms, blind doors, darkened
    tunnels—
We shared this legacy, in silence, during those
    father-final hours.

Untethered

That spring you were leaving
      ropes of oxygen
      coils of feeding tube
      strips of linen binding your wrists.

There was no calling you back
      as I rubbed your moist stone arms
      with thick towels
      and listened to your slender breath.

Too late, too late
      for words
      I sped my forgiveness
      to catch you at the rim of light.

      Now

Each spring I anoint your earth with holy salt
      write my prayer on linen strips
      fold and wedge them beneath
      your stone—a wailing wall.

After Life

My views of death and after-life
were Catechism simple.
We live.
We die.
We are punished.
We sit and are dazzled
by God all day.

Then I lived a line of life.

I concluded that days tick
like a metronome. And stop.
We make reparation
for our rust and dust;
then are swept
by a divinely-sleeved arm
into a perfect world,
where we do what we did on earth
flawlessly, endlessly, busily.

Then my father died.

The First Pressing

There is nothing sudden about death.
His last years were spent
in dying.
On his last day, I wasn't sure
which breath was his last.
Existence never stopped;
his spirit burned
like an intense blue flame
to light his way
to somewhere else.

His pain and cleansing
did not follow him
when he left the earth.
He does not sit idle
dazzled by God;
nor is he caught up
in frenetic activity.
He acts in concert with God
in things beyond imagination.

Seasoning

Generations have bloomed on my shoulder.
Many summers older, I cradled three sisters
who budded, windflower vines winding to the moon.

Like spring shoots, five babies of my own
leaned into me, curled their stubby toes
on the shelf of the palm of my hand.

In my early autumn, I wrapped
grandbabies in lullabies; rocked
them against my breast, past the harvest sky.

Now my shoulders sprout hen wings.
Hovering, I cover my mother,
try to shield her from the deep winter sting.

Earthbound

Early Alzheimer's Disease

I could slice you some moon
lace it with rum
serve it in a golden cup.
But you would reply
that it's not on your diet
and you prefer the Oreo
on your nursing home tray.

I could spread my Butterick pattern
across the clouds
cut and sew them into a robe.
But you would complain that you
don't have room in your tiny closet
or that it doesn't have a name tag
and besides, the faded chenille
is good enough for you.

Donna Wahlert

I could sail us on a star
to the Cotes du Rhone
to the Abbey at Tournus
where we could light a candle
kneel on stone
smoothed by a thousand years
of sandaled monks.
But you would blow out the mood
with heavy sighs about how you hate
the sauerkraut and weekly bingo.

I would spin the planets backward
to the time of Jane Austin
when we could laugh under lap robes
in a leather-lined carriage
and dance at an English ball.
But you would interrupt the music with a
Refrain—
how the staff is fattening you up
like Sunday's roasting hen
or how the lady piddled on your floor
five months ago.

The First Pressing

I would plant and tend an Eden
stroll through it with you
name the columbine
paint each honeysuckle.
But you would only see
the weeds and worms
and smell the dank compost.
You would prefer to stay as you are:
potted, root bound,
turned away from the sun.

Here Let Us

Late Middle Alzheimer's Disease

Here let us sit together
under the weeping beech
here let us talk about milk glass
chifforobes and elderberry wine
here let us soothe your ankles
swollen with childhood memories
we won't remind you that your mother
has been gone for thirty years
that the house you want to go
home to is no longer there
that your children are grown and gray
that you are the last of your friends
here let us drink our wintergreen tea
and talk about this primrose
the thin spaghetti you had for lunch
the nurse who brings you Hershey bars
here let us not dream about the days to come
here let us sing you your mother
here let us sing you your children
here let us sing you home.

Between Two Worlds

On the blurred cusp
between sleep and waking
I could not remember
what day it was,
where I was,
at what bus stop my life was waiting.
It was like surging through seas
with no compass,
speeding down highways
with no road signs,
spiraling down blackened storm clouds
with no horizon,
no thumbprint of the land below.
In that morning moment of panic
I lost my future, misplaced my past.
The present was frightening,
unsettling in its blindness.

Donna Wahlert

Was this what my mother felt
all through those sad nights
and anonymous days
those long years fevered
with senile dementia
when she could not remember
where she lived,
forgot that she had ever married,
could not recognize
her children around her?
Many times, on the edge of her bed,
my mother would ask me:
"Am I alive or dead?"
The question, always shocking,
recalled St. Paul's mystical words
to his disciples:
*"whether I was in the body or out of the body,
I do not know."*

This morning
that curious scripture in Corinthians
and my mother's startling question
were clear to me.
In that fearsome instant
between dream and waking
I too, flickered
between two worlds.

*2 Corinthians 12:3

The Long Good-Bye

Last Stages of Alzheimer's Disease

During the long years of my mother's Alzheimer's disease, there were many crises. At times, we thought she was near death. Death seemed most imminent in the ninth year when she fell and broke her hip. She was hospitalized and had surgery, but her health continued to deteriorate. She was so weak and ate so little over the next three weeks, that we summoned hospice. The hospice nurses too, thought that life might end sometime soon for our eighty-seven year old mother.

During this period of day-to-day waiting, an extraordinary thing occurred. Although it hadn't happened for years, my mother had moments of hazy lucidity, split seconds when she recognized us as her children again, specks of time when she realized she was sick and dying. We tried to be with her as much as possible and share these spurts of time when it was almost like having our mother back in the pre-Alzheimer's days.

Donna Wahlert

Family and friends whom she had not seen in years visited her to say their good-byes. A few were lucky enough to glimpse a special moment of clarity; most were not. Trying to smooth everything for her last journey, we asked Mom if there was anyone else that she needed to say good-bye to. She quietly replied, "Myself."

That answer, given in the ninth year of Alzheimer's disease, was so profound that I could not speak. I carried it with me turning it over in my mind and examining it like a rare jewel. I had read the books about near-death, about grief and loss, about saying good-bye, about the dying process. I realized the necessity of letting go, of separating from the loving people in one's life, from home and books, pets, bird song, flowers and the huge Maple.

But until my mother spoke it, I had never considered that we must say good-bye to that self that housed us, was us, for all those years. To the body that danced and cooked, made love and gave birth; to the mind that studied, analyzed, learned discernment; to the source of emotions that laughed and cried and prayed, and caught trails of wisdom.

The First Pressing

Despite her dementia, my mother taught me in this single response that not only must we say good-bye to what we *have* in this life, but we must say good-bye to what we have *been* in this life. It was a profound lesson, a wondrous gift.

Leaving This World For The Next

We summoned the hospital chaplain;
he did not answer his page.
We called the parish priest
to come anoint our dying mother.
He said he couldn't come just then.
We could not, would not wait.
My sisters and I said,
"We will anoint her ourselves."
Gathering around her bed,
we sang her favorite hymns,
prayed her litany of special prayers
that she had written down in a notebook.
We fingered the beads on her crystal rosary.
We shaped our own sacrament of the dying:
we signed her forehead with the cross
of ten years of Alzheimer's disease;
we blessed her whole body that had carried us,
worried about us, taught us, laughed with us.
We sealed her with the balm of our final care.
We caressed her paper-sheer hands,
stroked her brow, her cheek.
We kissed her.

The First Pressing

We sat on her bed, curling into her,
offering the warmth of our bodies
long past that last breath.

Reflection

We string our minutes together, rosary beads,
        and whisper life like a mantra
barely conscious of the individual stones
        not aware of the stringing, the pattern,
the meaning behind the automatic fingering.

Only when we crack open the moment
        shake out the seeds of past and present
and lay them in the sun like a jeweler
        do we see the splendor of each sand-spun
pearl and the grandeur of our design.

Triolet to My Five Children

As imperfect as I was
It's the best thing that I have ever done
Raised five children; calling to heaven
As every mother does
As imperfect as I was
We had love; we had fun
A nettlesome stone now and then
As imperfect as I was
It is still the best thing that I have ever done.

After His First Heart Attack

I know the placement
of your every freckle
the bend of each hair
the curve of your chin
the contour of each finger.
All I ask is time
To study them
Again and again.

Forty Years Are Not Enough

Forty years are not enough
to tell you how our love has grown.
In the halcyon honeymoon days,
we thought our love was at its peak.
But, oh, so little did we know
of mountain tops then.
We look down now
at what was merely a base camp.
True, the ascent was not a catapult.
We climbed and scaled smaller spires;
we slipped, dug in our clamps,
scrambled up again.
But each new attempt took us to a plateau
higher than before where we could look down
and see the peaks where we had been
and look up and see Olympian heights
still beckoning.
At forty years, we have reached a crest
—a comfortable place to rest—for now.
But just as honeymoon heights proved not enough,
the summit still awaits.

After His Second Heart Attack:
A Psalm

How many miracles can I ask for, O Lord?
How many times can I come to your door?
I have paced before your entryway so many times
that the carpet is threadbare.
You have always answered my knock
and given me the bread that I needed.
I have thanked you, but not enough.
My knees should be as tattered as the carpet.
Yet, here I am again, persistent,
like the woman with a hemorrhage
stubbornly asking to touch the hem of your garment.
All I want is to feel that linen woven with light
and implore you to heal my husband
and ask you to give me peace.
My heart feels so threadbare.

Upon Awakening

You cup my hand
against your cheek
on the pillow,
tilt your head
and kiss my wrist,
whisking away
all the worries
of today.

Explaining To My Children

To be planted in a box under layers of soil
would magnify my horror of closed-in space.
To be sifted and sealed in a ginger jar
would sentence me to a more confining jail.
But to be sprinkled on hill and wood and water,
bound only by a seamless veil of sky,
would allow me to linger a while
and melt back into the earth.

You ask where you could come to visit me—

You could
fathom me in the whistling poplar
and in the oak that holds its leaves
until spring;
in the pinkness of the foxglove
and in the river current
as it splits the states in two.

You could find me
in your mirror.
I am
the greenness in your eyes
the stubbornness of your hairline
the determination in your walk.

Index

A Catholic Woman Asks: Who is Priest? 94
A Snake As A Pet 18
A Three-Year-Old Visits 34
After His First Heart Attack 133
After His Second Heart Attack: A Psalm 135
After Life 117
An Astonishing Side Trip 57
Animal Blessing for the Feast of St. Francis of Assisi 73
Another Season 69
Attending the Birth of My Granddaughter 3
Ballooning Over Minnesota 48
Before My Grandson's Surgery 12
Between Two Worlds 124
Blessing For Family Reunion 81
Blessings in All Directions 7
Climbing Down the Rocky Mountains 35
Closing In 115
Colic 21
Concerning Dogs 52
Deer Domain 23
Dust 83
Earthbound 120
East meets West 61
Echoes 6
Eve 9
Evening Drama 54
Explaining To My Children 137
First Communion 25
Flora 37
Forty Years Are Not Enough 134

The First Pressing

Gabriel	113
Generations	44
God As Heat	47
Go Figure…	87
Hanna	15
Here Let Us	123
I come from a house with no floors.	90
I Wish I could Write a Poem About My Mother	77
In China During Christmas	111
In The Garden With My Grandson	55
Last Chance	88
Leaving This World For The Next	129
Lucy Conquers ALS	108
Making Way For the Interstate	50
Meditation at 7:00 a.m.	43
Music to My Ears	39
My Grandmother's Kitchen	79
Nine-Eleven	63
Nocturne	65
Novena	82
Observing Thanksgiving	74
Ode to Bread	58
Old Loves Revisited	85
On Folding Napkins For a Dinner Party	101
Putti	24
Reflection	131
Sacrament	11
Seasoning	119
Separation	40
Snowbirds	99
Sonnet To My Daughter on Her Twenty-First Birthday	76
Still Life	95
Storm Signals	54
Strands	104

Tea Time at Thomas Hardy's Cottage 19
The Barometer Plunges 20
The Curtain Falls 109
The Jelly Maker 106
The Long Good-Bye 126
The Mother Goose Prayer 16
The Quilters 75
The Transplant 45
This Mississippi 56
To A Lost Grandmother 92
To My Eurasian Grandchild 10
Triolet to a Spring Fawn 5
Triolet to My Five Children 132
Triolet To Sydney 14
Untethered 116
Upon Awakening 136
We Have Moved To A New House 31
Wedding Cake 59
When the Time Comes 103
Windchimes 26
Windfall in the Orchard 71

0-595-28959-2